EP Bible:
Old Testament
Levels 1-4

This book belongs to:

_____

Table of Contents

Lessons

Lesson 1

1. We're going to start the year off with reading one of the Gospels. We'll do this every year. This year we'll read Matthew and then we'll go back to the beginning and start reading in Genesis.
2. Read Matthew 1:18-24.
3. Tell the story to a parent.
4. This is the end of your work for this course for your first day. You are allowed to move at your own pace (this is homeschooling), but it's intended you complete one lesson a day.

Lesson 2

1. Read Matthew 2:1-12.
2. How do the wise men know that Jesus will be born in Bethlehem?
3. How did they know not to go and tell Herod about Jesus?
4. Check your answers.

Lesson 3

1. Read Matthew 3.
2. John tells the Pharisees that those who produce bad fruit will go to hell ("thrown into the fire"). What does He say about the kind of "fruit" they should produce? [Hint[1]]
3. John the Baptist didn't think he should be baptizing Jesus, but Jesus told him it was the right thing to do. Jesus gave us the example, and we are to follow in His footsteps and be baptized as well. It's not something to be afraid of. It marks the beginning of our life of following Jesus.
4. Check your answers.

Lesson 4

1. Read Matthew 4:1-11.
2. Tell a parent or older sibling how Satan tried to tempt Jesus and how Jesus responded to him.
3. Copy or memorize this part of Matthew 4:4: "Man does not live on bread alone, but on every word that comes from the mouth of God."

Lesson 5

1. Read Matthew 5:1-12.
2. Who is blessed? You can insert the word "happy" instead of blessed.
3. What do they receive?
4. How can being persecuted and being lied about make you happy?
5. Check your answers.

Lesson 6

1. Read Matthew 6:1-15.
2. Copy Matthew 6:9-13. Hang it up where you will see it and work on memorizing it this week.

---

[1] verse 8

Lesson 7

1. Read Matthew 7:7-14 and 7:24-29.
2. How can you be wise like the man whose house didn't fall? [Hint[2]]
3. Check your answers.

Lesson 8

1. Read Matthew 8:1-13.
2. Let's compare and contrast these stories. That means to find what they have in common and what's different about them.
3. What are some things that they have in common?
4. What are some things that are different?
5. Check your answers.
6. Did you find some that I didn't?

Lesson 9* (Note that an asterisk * indicates that there is a worksheet on this lesson)

1. Read Matthew 9:18-37.
2. What is one reason Jesus healed everyone who came to Him? (hint: verse 36)
3. *On the worksheet, write on each line someone you should have compassion on. "S" could be soldiers, "p" could be people without homes, or they could just be names. (These Bible worksheets are in the Ancient History Theme Printables workbook if you have bought that. They can also be printed all at once as a packet. Go to the course page of the website and look for "Worksheets" towards the top.)

Lesson 10

1. Read Matthew 10:1-8.
2. How many of the 12 apostles can you name? If you can't name them all, go back and find who you are missing.
3. The last sentence in this section is, "You have received freely, so give freely." What does that mean?
4. What have you been given that you should be giving?

Lesson 11

1. Read Matthew 11:2-10.
2. Jesus quotes a prophecy from the Old Testament book of Malachi. He says the prophecy is about John the Baptist. What does it say John was going to do?
3. In your reading today, you read that John has his disciples ask Jesus if He is the Messiah. Jesus doesn't say yes or no. He answers that he has healed the blind, the lame, the deaf and the leper and that He is preaching the gospel (good news) to the poor. Why did he say those things? Jesus was telling John that other Old Testament prophecies were being fulfilled. The Old Testament prophets said that a Messiah or Savior would come and heal and preach the gospel to the poor.

---

[2] verse 24

Read Isaiah 35:5-6. Read Isaiah 61:1. Do those verses sound like what Jesus told John? Do you think John understood Jesus' message?

4. Check your answers.

Lesson 12

1. Read Matthew 12:1-13.
2. What were the Pharisees accusing Jesus and his disciples of doing?
3. Jesus shows the Pharisees that they are hypocrites because they would help a sheep on the Sabbath but not a person. This is one way you can tell if something is from God or not. God cares about people. the Pharisees didn't care about the man who needed healing. They cared about their rules. They were proud of their sacrifice to not work on the Sabbath. But Jesus told them that they were not doing what God wanted, that God wanted them to love others. That's what Jesus meant he said, "I want mercy and not sacrifice."
4. Copy the sentence, "I want mercy and not sacrifice."
5. Tell someone the story you read today and explain what it means that God wants mercy and not sacrifice.
6. Check your answers.

Lesson 13

1. Read Matthew 13:1-9, 18-23.
2. Draw a picture of the parable and then explain to someone what the picture means.

Lesson 14

1. Read Matthew 14:13-21.
2. Tell a parent or older sibling what happened in this story.
3. God can take whatever you have to offer and turn it into a big blessing. But first you have to offer what you have. What do you have that you could give? It could be money or food or toys, or it could be things like time and love. You could stop by the home of an elderly neighbor and say good morning. What else could you give that God could turn into a big blessing for you and others?

Lesson 15

1. Read Matthew 15:1-18.
2. In some other parts of the world, being clean is THE most important thing. For example, Muslims won't pray unless they wash themselves first. In Muslim countries being called "dirty" is one of the worst insults. What does Jesus say makes you "unclean?" Explain to a parent or ask if you don't understand what Jesus is saying.

Lesson 16

1. Read Matthew 16:5-12.
2. Jesus is using **figurative** language. That means that he is not speaking plainly. He's making word pictures. In this section he warns the disciples about the yeast of the Pharisees and the Sadducees. Yeast is what you put in bread to make it rise. You put a little bit into the flour, and

it gets through the whole dough to make it rise. Jesus doesn't mean "make sure you don't get their yeast on you." What is Jesus really warning the disciples about? (answer: Jesus was warning about what the religious leaders taught.)

Lesson 17

1. Read Matthew 17:24-27.
2. This is a fun story. Remember that earlier, when Jesus was a teenager, he had called the temple "his father's house." Here Jesus is saying that He doesn't have to pay the tax because it is His father's house, and fathers don't collect tax from their sons.
3. What does Jesus do to pay the tax?
4. Can God always provide the money you need?
5. There are many, many stories of Christians getting the money they needed at just the right moment, from finding five dollars stuck to your shoe while walking down the street, to having an angel hand you the money. God has plenty of ways of providing. Trust Him to do it!

Lesson 18

1. Read Matthew 18:21-35.
2. Tell a parent or older sibling what happened in the story.
3. What is the lesson of this story?
4. Check your answers.

Lesson 19

1. Read Matthew 19:16-30.
2. How do we know the rich man wasn't really loving his neighbor as himself?
3. Check your answers.

Lesson 20

1. Read Matthew 20:25-28.
2. Why did Jesus come?
3. Verse 28 commands, "Be like Jesus." How can you live your life to serve others? What are some things you can do every day? What is something you can aspire to do (dream about doing or work towards doing) for others when you are older?
4. Check your answers.

Lesson 21

1. Read Matthew 21:1-17.
2. In this section we see several more prophecies from the Old Testament fulfilled. God knew exactly what was going to happen. The donkeys were prepared and waiting for him even though the owner didn't know it! You don't have to try and do big things for God. All you have to do is be willing and ready to obey Him.
3. Do you know why Jesus was so angry in the temple? What did he call it?
4. People who were not Jews were not allowed inside the temple. They were only allowed in an outer court area of the temple. That's the place that was given to them to pray. But Jews had set

up tables for selling the animals that people use for sacrifice and sold money to people who didn't have the special coins used in the temple. They were making money off of people coming to worship God. Plus, they were making it so that people who weren't Jews had no place to pray.

5. Check your answers.

Lesson 22

1. Read Matthew 22:1-14.
2. Can you tell the story? What happened?
3. This is a parable, a story that has another meaning. Jesus wasn't really telling them about a king. Who is the real king and the king's son? What do you think?
4. The people who ignore the king's request to come to the dinner or who kill the king's servants are the Jews. The servants are God's prophets. As a whole group, the Jews didn't listen to the prophets and even killed some of them.
5. Then the king invites everyone else, meaning those who aren't Jews. Many show up. One is thrown out because he's not wearing wedding clothes. What do you think that really means?
6. Check your answers.

Lesson 23

1. Read Matthew 23:1-15.
2. What are the Pharisees like?
3. I wonder what pastors and priests who are called "Father" or "Reverend" think when they read verses 8-10.
4. The most important thing to learn from this is that God cares what's in your heart. If your heart is good (you love God and love others), then you will do good. If you are only acting good on the outside, eventually your evil heart will show. You can't pretend forever.
5. Check your answers.

Lesson 24

1. Read Matthew 24:1-14.
2. The disciples want to know when the end will come, when Jesus will come back and rule. We are still wondering, wanting to know!
3. Jesus doesn't tell them. He tells them that people will try and fool them, saying that He has already come back. What other command does He give them? "Don't…"?
4. He says there will be wars, famine, earthquakes, and Christians will be put in prison and killed. But we aren't to be afraid! It's all part of God's plan and He is only allowing it to happen to get His Church holy, ready to be with Him.
5. It says many will turn away from their faith because they will be afraid. We will obey whomever we fear. We need to fear God alone. He's the only leader who wants to do what's best for us instead of for himself.
6. Pray and ask God to help you not be afraid.
7. Check your answers.

Lesson 25

    1. Read Matthew 25:31-46.
    2. When you help people or ignore people, do you ever think about Jesus? When have you acted like a sheep? When have you acted like a goat?
    3. What are things you can do to be a sheep?

Lesson 26

    1. Read Matthew 26:47-56.
    2. Jesus says he could have asked for help and His Father would have send an army of angels. Why doesn't Jesus want an army of angels to rescue Him?
    3. Check your answers.

Lesson 27

    1. Read Matthew 27:11-26.
    2. What does the crowd yell?
    3. What did the crowd yell one week earlier?
    4. Check your answers.

Lesson 28

    1. Read Matthew 28.
    2. I met a Jewish woman once who told me Jesus' disciples took His body away while the guards were sleeping. It made me smile because her thinking that just proved the Bible true. Why? [Hint[3]]
    3. What's wrong with the guards' story?
    4. Check your answers.

Lesson 29

    1. We finished reading the Gospel of Matthew. Gospel means "good news." What is the good news that Matthew tell us?

Lesson 30

    1. Read Genesis 1.
    2. *Do the Creation circles worksheet. Draw or write what God created each of the first four days of creation.

Lesson 31

    1. Read Genesis 2.
    2. *Fill in circles for Day 5 (birds and fish), Day 6 (other animals and people), and Day 7 (holy).

---

[3] verse 15

Lesson 32

1. Read Genesis 3.
2. Tell the story or act it out.
3. Who does Eve blame?
4. Who does Adam blame?
5. Check your answers.
6. The Bible says, "If we confess our sins, He is faithful to forgive us" (1 John 1:9). We need to confess (tell) our sins to God to have them forgiven. Don't be like Adam and Eve. Admit that you did something wrong and ask forgiveness.

Lesson 33

1. Read Genesis 4:1-16.
2. What does God say in verses 6 and 7?
3. He tells Cain he is only sad and angry because he did wrong. If he had done what is right (offered God the first and best things he had grown), then he wouldn't be sad and angry. Sin made him sad and angry. He's not sad that he sinned against God. He's pouting. What does God say sin wants to do to Cain?
4. Cain had to make a choice right there. Would he conquer sin or let sin conquer him? Who won?
5. What are ways you can conquer sin?
6. Check your answers.

Lesson 34

1. Read Genesis 6:5-22.
2. Why did God choose to send the flood?
3. Why did God choose Noah to be safe?
4. Check your answers.

Lesson 35

1. Read Genesis 7.
2. Noah built that boat for a long time. It just sat there on dry ground. He trusted God and obeyed God even though it seemed like nothing was happening. How long before the flood did Noah know when it was coming?
3. Who was saved? Who was in the ark?
4. How long did the flood last?
5. What questions do you have about this story? I wonder what they ate on the ark. What do you wonder?
6. Check your answers.

Lesson 36

1. Read Genesis 8:1-4, 13-21, Genesis 9:3-4, 11-15.
2. Find Mount Ararat on the map on the next page.
3. What were the "clean" animals for?
4. After the flood, what could they now eat?

5. Do you think God told them to be vegetarians before the flood so that Noah's family wouldn't kill and eat the animals God was trying to preserve? (Just wondering.)
6. What is God's covenant (promise)? What is the sign to remember His promise?
7. Check your answers.

Public domain; https://commons.wikimedia.org/wiki/File:Ararat-Location.png

Lesson 37

1. Read Genesis 11:1-8 and 27-31.
2. Read Genesis 12:1-8.
3. Why did God confuse their language? [Hint[4]]
4. How is Abram (later he is named Abraham) related to Lot? Can you figure it out?
5. What did God command Abram?
6. What did God promise Abram?
7. Check your answers.

Lesson 38

1. Read Genesis 13:8-18.
2. What city did Lot choose to live near?
3. What was wrong in the city where he chose to live?
4. Check your answers.

Lesson 39

1. Read Genesis 15:1-7, 13-16.
2. What does God promise Abram?
3. What was Abram's right reaction?
4. What does God say is going to happen to Abram's descendants for 400 years?

---

[4] Genesis 11:6

5. Check your answers.

Lesson 40

1. Read Genesis 17:1-17.
2. What new names did they receive?
3. What's the answer going to be to the questions in verse 17?
4. Check your answers.

Lesson 41

1. Read Genesis 18:17-33.
2. What is happening in this chapter? What does God plan on doing? What is Abraham doing?
3. Will God destroy the righteous with the wicked?
4. Read Genesis 19:15-26. This is the next morning. The angels are sent to destroy the city and to get Lot and his family out first.
5. What happens to Lot's wife when she doesn't obey the angel's directions?
6. What lessons can you learn from these chapters?
7. Check your answers.

Lesson 42

1. Read Genesis 21:1-7.
2. Sarah says that everyone who hears about this will laugh. Did you laugh? Sometimes we don't stop to think about Bible stories being real stories that happened to real people. Can you image a woman who is A LOT older than your grandmother being pregnant and having a baby after never having a baby her whole life and without doctors and special treatments, etc.? It is pretty crazy! Even with doctors and technology, no one has come even close to having a baby as old as Sarah did.
3. Read Genesis 22:1-18.
4. This is a really important story. Here are some things to remember.
5. God does test us. When we are faced with something really hard, it shows what is really in our hearts. If God just gave us perfect lives, we would love Him for selfish reasons. We need to love God for who He really is. He is love; He is kind; He is just; He is powerful; He knows everything; He is in control; He is patient; He is faithful; He is trustworthy…What else do you know about who God is?
6. God never asks us to do something He wasn't willing to do Himself. This is one big example. God did give up His only Son to be killed for us. God never wanted Issac to be killed. He only wanted to see obedience in the heart of Abraham.
7. Abraham will be blessed. His children will be blessed. The whole world will be blessed because…? [Hint[5]]
8. Check your answers.

Lesson 43

1. Read Genesis 24.

---

[5] verse 18

2. Did you notice that God answered the servant's prayer before he even prayed?
3. Do you find it weird that Isaac and Rebekah get married without knowing each other first? In many parts of the world, a marriage arranged by parents is normal. The two are often given the choice, yes or no, but they may have only been just introduced to the person. I have never known anyone to say no (even when the other person is not attractive at all) because they respect the choice of their families.

Lesson 44

1. Read Genesis 25:19-34.
2. What are the names of Isaac's and Rebekah's sons?
3. Who was their grandfather?
4. What bad thing did Esau do?
5. Birth rights are something that were important historically. In many places throughout history the oldest son received all of the father's land and property. It was of great value to have the rights of the first born. Esau didn't value it and gave it away for food.
6. I want you to notice one more thing. God had it planned from the beginning that Jacob would be the "father of Israel," not Esau. It didn't matter that Esau had been born first. Lots and lots of times in the Bible you will see God choose not the first and the "best" (according to the way people see it), but He will more often choose the last and least important to do His work, and then they become very important.
7. Check your answers.

Lesson 45

1. Read Genesis 28:10-22.
2. What did Jacob dream?
3. What did God promise him?
4. What did Jacob promise God?
5. Check your answers.

Lesson 46

1. Read Genesis 29:10-35. Jacob has gone to his uncle's place to find a wife.
2. At the end of this chapter, how many sons does Leah have?
3. Jesus is born from the family line of the last of Leah's sons. Who was Jesus' great, great, great, great, great,.....grandfather?
4. Rachel eventually has two sons, including Joseph, who you probably know about. Leah has two more sons. Rachel and Leah also give their maids to be like wives to Jacob. They end up having four sons between the two of them. So, how many sons does Jacob have?
5. When the Bible talks about the tribes of Israel, they are the family groups started by each of these sons.
6. Check your answers.

Lesson 47

1. Read Genesis 31:1-21.
2. What does Jacob do?

3. What does Rachel do?
4. Why would they believe a god is powerful if it can be picked up and stolen?
5. Check your answers.

Lesson 48

1. Read Genesis 37:1-11 and 19-36.
2. What were Joseph's dreams?
3. Why were his brothers mad?
4. Who wanted to save Joseph?
5. Who ended up being Joseph's owner?
6. Check your answers.

Lesson 49

1. Read Genesis 39.
2. What did God do for Joseph?
3. What was his job?
4. Potiphar's wife wanted Joseph to act like a husband toward her. Joseph refuses, but he makes the mistake of being alone with her. What happens to Joseph because of her lie?
5. Check your answers.

Lesson 50

1. Read Genesis 40.
2. Who was sent to jail?
3. They both had dreams. What did Joseph do?
4. Check your answers.

Lesson 51

1. Read Genesis 41:1-16, 25-27.
2. What was Pharaoh's dream and what did it mean?
3. Check your answers.

Lesson 52

1. Read Genesis 41:41-57.
2. What did Joseph do to prepare for the famine?
3. What did he do once the Egyptians felt the famine and asked Pharaoh for food?
4. Check your answers.

Lesson 53

1. Read chapter 42:1-26.
2. Who came to Egypt?
3. What does Joseph accuse them of?
4. What happened to make Joseph remember his dream?

5. Check your answers.

Lesson 54

1. Read Genesis 43:11-32. Israel has finally agreed to let them go back to Egypt to buy more grain after they had already eaten all the grain they had brought. He took so long to agree because he was worried about Benjamin, who had to travel with them this time.
2. Now instead of favoring Joseph because he was Rachel's son, he favors Benjamin because he was Rachel's son. Israel/Jacob even left Simeon in prison all this time while they used up all of the grain instead of sending the brothers back right away to get him out of prison. All because he valued Benjamin more than Simeon. But the brothers act differently toward Benjamin. They are no longer jealous. They understand and are treating him as more important, saying they will place his life above theirs.

Lesson 55

1. Read Genesis 44:1-11, 18-19, 33-34.
2. What happened? What did Joseph sneak into Benjamin's sack?
3. He is testing them to see how they will treat his mother's son, Benjamin. He sees they have changed their hearts and do not treat Benjamin the way they treated him.
4. Who offers to be a slave instead of Benjamin?
5. Check your answers.

Lesson 56

1. Read Genesis 45:1-10.
2. The brothers sold him, but who does Joseph say "sent" him?
3. Some people say God only does the "good" stuff. He doesn't send the bad stuff in our lives. But here Joseph is saying that God was in control of all the "bad" that happened to him. The thing is, when God is in control, He works it all out so it ends up being for your good.
4. Check your answers.

Lesson 57

1. Read Genesis 46:2-4.
2. What promises did God give Jacob?
3. Read Genesis 47:1-6.
4. Where did the Israelites settle?
5. Check your answers.

Lesson 58

1. Read Genesis 50:15-26.
2. What were Joseph's brothers afraid of?
3. Joseph tells the brothers that God had used his coming to Egypt for good and saved many lives. How did God save many lives through Joseph's being sold as a slave?
4. Check your answers.

Lesson 59

1. Read Exodus 1:8-13, 22.
2. Did you notice we started a new book? Exodus. EX in the beginning of a word means *out,* like in the word EXit. In Exodus the Israelites are going to come out of Egypt. The main character of the story now is going to be Moses. This is where his story is going to begin.
3. What did the new Pharaoh do to the Hebrews?
4. A long time passes…
5. Read Exodus 2:1-10.
6. Moses' mother hides him by the river. Now she must have hidden him near Pharaoh's palace because Pharaoh's daughter finds him and feels bad for him and wants to take care of him. And one of my favorite things in the whole Bible is that Pharaoh's daughter hires Moses' own mother to take care of him!
7. Check your answers.

Lesson 60

1. Read Exodus 2:11-25.
2. Moses sees the Israelites being treated wrongly. He tries to save one himself. How did he do it?
3. He made things worse instead of better. God is going to use Moses to save, or deliver, the Israelites from the Egyptians, but it's not going to be by the power of man.
4. Moses ends up living with the Midianites and marries one of them.
5. This is happening about 40 years later. Read Exodus 3:1-10.
6. We'll read more about this day.
7. Check your answers.

Lesson 61

1. Read Exodus 3:7-22.
2. Tell someone what God's plan is. What are all of the instructions to Moses?

Lesson 62

1. Read Exodus 4:1-17.
2. Moses is worried that the Israelites won't believe him and he's worried that he won't be able to speak well. What does God do to help him?
3. Check your answers.

Lesson 63

1. Read Exodus 5:1-9, 22-23.
2. What was Pharaoh's response when Moses and Aaron asked him to let them go for a few days?
3. Moses is upset because God sent him to deliver his people from the Egyptians but instead he made things worse! He doesn't know what's about to happen.
4. Check your answers.

Lesson 64

1. Read Exodus 7:14-24.
2. What was the first plague God sent to change Pharaoh's mind?
3. Notice that Pharaoh's magicians, who practice evil magic, could also turn water into blood. Notice that God allowed them only to make the plague worse! They couldn't make it better! If they truly had power like God's, they could have turned it back into water. Only God could end the plague.
4. Check your answers.

Lesson 65

1. There is a plague of frogs and a plague of gnats all over Egypt. Pharaoh's magicians can make more frogs, but they can't make the dust turn into gnats like God did. The Israelites suffered through these first plagues it seemed. I'm sure after those plagues, the Israelites had changed their minds about Moses and believed that God was using him to rescue them from the Egyptians.
2. Read Exodus 8:20-30.
3. What did God do differently this time to show that He was in control over the land?
4. Check your answers.

Lesson 66

1. Read Exodus 9:1-7.
2. What plague did God send?
3. How did God show that He was the God of the Hebrews?
4. In the rest of the chapter God sends a plague of boils, which are sores on your body, and a plague of hail.
5. Check your answers.

Lesson 67

1. Next came a plague of locusts. Then…
2. Read Exodus 10:21-29.
3. What plague is God going to send next?
4. How will God treat the Hebrews differently from the Egyptians?
5. What does Moses agree with at the end of the chapter?
6. Check your answers.

Lesson 68

1. Read Exodus 12:1-16.
2. What was the last plague?
3. When death passed over the Israelites because of the lamb's blood, that night we call the Passover. Death passed over them. Jesus died during the Jewish holiday of Passover. His last meal was the Passover supper and then he was killed. That's why we call Jesus the Lamb of God. He was our Passover lamb. His blood covers us and makes it so death can pass over us

and not touch us. Many things in the Old Testament reflect what is going to happen in the New Testament. Sometimes they seem so different, but they really are a perfect match!

4. Check your answers.

Lesson 69

1. Read Exodus 14:5-28.
2. What happened?
3. Check your answers.

Lesson 70

1. Read Exodus 15:19-27.
2. What test does the Lord give the Israelites?
3. Check your answers.

Lesson 71

1. Read Exodus 16:1-4, 11-23.
2. When the Israelites were hungry, what did they do?
3. What did God provide for them?
4. This type of bread the Israelites named manna, and they ate it every day for forty years until they came to the land God promised them.
5. Check your answers.

Lesson 72

1. Read Exodus 17:1-13.
2. How were they testing the Lord?
3. What did Moses have to do for the Israelites to win against the Amalekites?
4. Check your answers.

Lesson 73

1. Read Exodus 19:16-25.
2. What is this talking about? Moses is talking to God on Mount Sinai (pronounced "sigh-nigh"). Only Aaron is allowed to come along. Everyone else must be set apart as holy — they had to clean their clothes and make sure they didn't do anything wrong just so that they could stand near the mountain. Anyone who touched the mountain would die. We'll read more about this later, how God is holy and people cannot just go into His presence. That's the most powerful thing that Jesus did. His death and resurrection make it so that we can be made holy and can go into God's presence. On the mountain, God is going to give the law, the Ten Commandments, to Moses.

Lesson 74

1. Read Exodus 20:1-12.
2. *What are the Ten Commandments? Fill in the worksheet. You will finish it in the next lesson.

Lesson 75

    1. Read Exodus 20:13-24.
    2. Finish your worksheet from Lesson 74.

Lesson 76

    1. What comes next is the Law. We are not going to read the whole law given to the Israelites. There are more than 600 laws. They cover all sorts of things. Things like, "If your cow wanders away and falls into a hole on someone else's land…" and tells you what should happen to be fair.
    2. Read Exodus 23:20-33.
    3. What are the Israelites told not to do? [Hint6]
    4. What are they promised if they obey and worship God? [Hint7]
    5. What do verses 32 and 33 say they shouldn't do? What happens if they do?

Lesson 77

    1. Read Exodus 24. Be on the lookout for strange and unusual things.
    2. What did you notice that was strange and unusual?
    3. What do the Israelites promise to do? [Hint8]
    4. Check your answers.

Lesson 78

    1. Up on the mountain God gives Moses instructions for building him a place to live among the Israelites. It's called a tabernacle. There are six chapters on instructions for how to build it, what to put inside it (for offering sacrifices and for honoring God's presence) and for who can approach it and how. Below is a picture of what the tabernacle was like.
    2. Read Exodus 32:1-8 and 31-35.
    3. What sin did the Israelites commit?
    4. How did God punish them?
    5. Check your answers.

---

6 verse 24
7 verse 25
8 verse 7

22

Lesson 79

1. Read Exodus 34:1-14, 29-32.
2. Who wrote the Ten Commandments on the tablets? [Hint[9]]
3. What are some of the ways that God describes Himself? [Hint[10]]

Lesson 80

1. Read Leviticus 6.
2. Did you notice? We moved into new book. The rest of Exodus repeated all of the directions for the tabernacle while the people built it. God was very specific in how it should be done, what colors, what sizes. The tabernacle, the arc and the mercy seat were where God dwelt among the Israelites. And just like when God's presence was on the mountain, anyone not invited and not made holy could not go into the tabernacle, or they would die. That's what Jesus did for us. He makes us holy so that we can be in God's presence. That doesn't mean we get to sin and still be with God. It means that we can be holy through repentance and through the forgiveness we are offered, because Jesus took our punishment for us by dying on the cross.
3. In Leviticus we read about many more of the laws. In this chapter it talks about some of the offerings they are required to make. When someone sinned, something had to be sacrificed, an animal was killed, so that the sin could be forgiven. In the New Testament we read, "The wages

---

[9] verse 1
[10] verses 6 and 7

23

of sin is death." Death is the payment sin requires. That's what Jesus did for us. He made the payment. We don't sacrifice animals anymore because Jesus was the final sacrifice, great enough for all of us.

4. When an offering was made, sometimes for sin, sometimes to say thank you, sometimes to celebrate a holiday, part of the animal was burnt (all the fat–God was keeping them healthy!) and part of the animal was given to the priest for him and his family to eat, and the rest the person making the offering got to keep/eat. There are very specific rules for all of it, which of course, the Israelites will soon break!

Lesson 81

1. The next few chapters are about the different types of sacrifices and Aaron and his sons making the sacrifices and offerings to God. Remember, there are specific rules for what they are supposed to do. If they feared and honored God, they would follow all of the rules. Then this happens…
2. Read Leviticus 10:1-3.
3. These are the rules God set for the Israelites for what they could eat.
4. What does the New Testament say about these dietary laws? Mark 7:18-19; Acts 10:9-16
5. The second one shows that the disciples didn't just give up their diet that they had been trained on since youth. The second one, the vision, was used by God to teach Peter that God could "clean" a non-Jew. Just after this, Peter goes to the home of a non-Jew, a Gentile, and preaches the gospel. Before, he wouldn't have even gone into the home of a Gentile because it was "unclean." But both of these show that the power of God is not found in food. Eating certain foods doesn't make us "unclean", unholy. Sin is what makes us unholy.

Lesson 82

1. What we skipped was a long list of rules for the Israelites to live by.
2. Read Leviticus 23.
3. This is a list of holidays the Israelites are to remember each year. You remember Passover, right? The Day of Atonement is when the Israelites' sins are forgiven when a sacrifice is made on their behalf. They are to live in little huts for a week during the Festival of Booths.

Lesson 83

1. Read Leviticus 25:11-28.
2. What does God say in verse 23?
3. What do you have that you don't really own, that really belongs to God? Ask your parents about it.
4. Check your answers.

Lesson 84

1. Read Leviticus 26:1-17. (audio)
2. What are some of the blessings promised to them when they obey?
3. What are some the punishments promised them when they disobey?

Lesson 85

1. Read Numbers 11:1-23, 31-34.
2. What did the Israelites do wrong?
3. How did God punish them?
4. Check your answers.

Lesson 86

1. Did you notice we are in a new book now? It's called Numbers. Can you guess why? Yep, there are a lot of numbers in the book. They count up everyone by family and keep records of everything. This is all significant as a record of history, but it's not terribly exciting.
2. Read Numbers 12.
3. Remember that Aaron, Moses, and Miriam are brothers and sister. How are Aaron and Miriam feeling?
4. What happened to Miriam?
5. What was special about Moses?
6. Check your answers.

Lesson 87

1. The Israelites have reached part of the land that God promised them. Moses sends spies into the land to see what's there.
2. Read Numbers 13:17-33.
3. Who wasn't afraid of the people in the land and said that they should go take the land?
4. Why is everyone else afraid?
5. Stand up. Look down at your feet and picture a grasshopper. The Israelites said that's what they felt like next to the people who lived there. There were giants living there, like Goliath was a giant, but saying they were like grasshoppers next to them was definitely an exaggeration.
6. Check your answers.

Lesson 88

1. This is a bit of a long one today. Be patient to read it. Read Numbers 14:1-10, 26-45. This starts right after the Israelites hear that there are giants living in the land they are supposed to go conquer and live in.
2. What are they saying?
3. What do they want to do to Joshua and Caleb?
4. What's their punishment?
5. When they realize they are going to be punished, they say, "Oh, we'll obey now," and they go up to fight, but that wasn't what they were supposed to do. It was too late. They got beaten in the battle.
6. Check your answers.

Lesson 89

1. Read Numbers 16:1-7, 28-35, 41-50.

2. These men were sons of Levi. That means they were Levites. They were the tribe chosen to care for the tabernacle and all related duties. Only specially chosen ones could be priests and enter the tabernacle to offer sacrifices and be in God's presence. They thought they were just as good as Aaron. They said, "The Lord is with us too, so we can present an offering to the Lord too."
3. They are all killed.
4. Do you have any guess why the Israelites didn't fear God after those men were killed? We know they didn't because they complained that Moses and Aaron had killed the Levites, when God was the one who had done it.
5. Then God punishes the Israelites and sends a plague. Thousands die until Aaron makes a sacrifice so that they can be forgiven.
6. These stories should teach you the fear of the Lord. He is holy and all-powerful and we can't treat Him just any way we please.

Lesson 90

1. Read Numbers 17.
2. What does God do to teach the Israelites who He has chosen so that they will stop complaining about their leaders?
3. Check your answers.

Lesson 91

1. Read Numbers 20:1-13.
2. You read that Miriam, Moses' sister, died. Later in the chapter Aaron dies.
3. The Israelites are complaining again about food and say it would have been better to have been killed than to die of thirst. Why don't they believe God will provide for them?!
4. What instruction does God give Moses?
5. What does Moses do?
6. Because Moses didn't treat God as holy (by disobeying what God had said), Moses and Aaron are told they will not be allowed to enter the Promised Land they have been leading the Israelites toward for 40 years. (It would have been a short journey, but they were forced to wander in the desert for 40 years because they didn't believe God would help them defeat the giants.)
7. Check your answers.

Lesson 92

1. The Israelites defeat one of the groups of people living in Canaan. Another group, the Moabites, are afraid. Their king, Balak, tries to get God on their side by asking Balaam to curse the Israelites.
2. Read Numbers 22:7-34.
3. God tells Balaam not to go with them. But when Balak's officials push him, he goes and asks God again. God is not pleased that Balaam was still willing to go with them after He had told Balaam no. What does God do to show Balaam He is angered?
4. What keeps Balaam from being killed by the angel?
5. What do you think makes this a famous story from the Bible?
6. Check your answers.

Lesson 93

1. Read Numbers 27. (audio)
2. This may not seem a significant chapter, but I wanted to point out something. It was really remarkable to have these daughters get the right to inherit land. Their father had died and he had no sons. God gives the land ownership to the man's daughters. While men seem to rule everything and get all the rights, God doesn't leave the women without hope. He provides for them and is thoughtful of them at all times.
3. Moses is about to die. Who does he pass on leadership responsibilities to?
4. Check your answers.

Lesson 94

1. We come to the book of Deuteronomy. In this book there is a retelling of Israel's history.
2. Read Deuteronomy 6.
3. Memorize Deuteronomy 6:4-5.
4. What promises does God give them if they obey? [Hint[11]]

Lesson 95

1. The whole book of Deuteronomy Moses is giving a speech. He reminds the Israelites of how God has taken care of them and of all of the promises He has made. He also reminds them of the laws and the consequences of disobeying. Towards the end he presents everyone with a choice. What is the choice?
2. Read Deuteronomy 30:11-20.
3. What is the choice?
4. We have the same choice today. We've already broken God's laws, but we can ask for forgiveness because of Jesus' death for us. And we can ask for the Holy Spirit to fill us and help us live according to God's Word.
5. Check your answers.

Lesson 96

1. Moses dies and Joshua becomes Israel's leader. He sends spies into Jericho and then leads all of Israel across the Jordan River.
2. Find the Jordan and Jericho on the map. The Jordan runs between the Sea of Galilee (the small body of water about a third of the way down the map) and the Dead Sea (the large body of water at the bottom of the map). Jericho is just north of the Dead Sea.
3. Read Joshua 2:1-14 and Joshua 3:14-17.
4. How does Israel cross the Jordan?
5. Check your answers.

---

[11] verses 2, 3 and 24

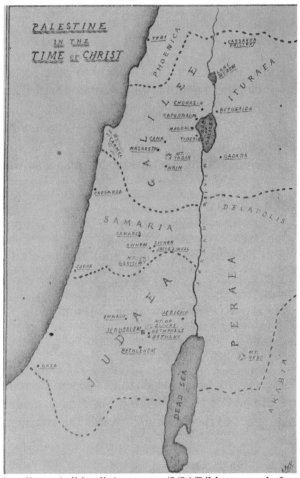

Public domain; https://upload.wikimedia.org/wikipedia/commons/8/84/Bible_manual._Introductory_course_on_the_Bible%2C_for_teachers_training_classes_and_Bible_classes_%281922%29_%2814586262848%29.jpg)

Lesson 97

1. Read Joshua 6:1-20.
2. What did they have to do in order to make the wall fall down?
3. Check your answers.

Lesson 98

1. Read Joshua 7:1-21.
2. What happens when they go to attack Ai?
3. Why?
4. Who broke God's command?
5. He is stoned to death because he disobeyed.
6. Check your answers.

Lesson 99

1. Read Joshua 10:1-15.
2. Five kings join together to attack. God tells Joshua that he will win. They surprise-attack them.
3. What does Joshua say to the sun?

4. Joshua was asking that night wouldn't fall until the battle was over. We don't know how God did it, but He did. Maybe the Lord provided the light Himself for the Israelites that day, to make it light all night. Or, maybe He broke the laws of physics that He created (like when He made an ax float). If God spoke the universe into existence, then he can control it by His word as well.
5. Check your answers.

Lesson 100

1. Read Joshua 24:1-21.
2. Joshua is about to die. He reminds Israel what God has done for them.
3. What does verse 12 say that God did for them?
4. What does everyone promise?
5. Check your answers.

Lesson 101

1. Read Judges 2.
2. You'll see that we've started a new book. Joshua dies and they don't have a leader except the Lord.
3. What do they do?
4. What is their punishment for breaking their side of the covenant?
5. When another nation defeats them, what is God going to do to help them?
6. Check your answers.

Lesson 102

1. Read Judges 4:1-9, 23-24.
2. The first verse mentions Ehud. He was the previous judge of Israel. Israel sins, God punishes them, they cry out to God for help, God sends a judge to deliver them and teach them again what is right and wrong.
3. Who is the newest judge? (It says "leader," but you can read what her job was. She acted as a judge. She told the people what was right and wrong.)
4. Check your answers.

Lesson 103

1. Read Judges 6:1-10, 36-40.
2. What did the Israelites do again?
3. What happened to them?
4. Anyone remember hearing about the Midianites before?
5. God chooses a man named Gideon to be the next deliverer and judge of Israel. How does Gideon feel about that?
6. Check your answers.

Lesson 104

1. Read Judges 7:1-21.
2. How many Israelites fought?

3. God showed them that it wasn't their strength that won battles, but His.
4. What trick did they do to make the Midianites think there were a lot more of them than there really were?
5. Check your answers.

Lesson 105

1. Read Judges 14:5-20.
2. Gideon has died and many other judges have ruled as Israel is in constant need of saving because they keep disobeying God.
3. Samson is the next chosen deliverer of Israel. He falls in love with a Philistine woman. Israelites aren't supposed to marry non-Israelites, but he does and God uses it as a way to get the Philistines, who at the time are ruling over Israel.
4. How do we know Samson is a strong man (in the power of God)?
5. Even though he was the strongest man, who was able to get the secret from him?
6. Why did he tell her?
7. Be careful whom you marry!
8. Check your answers.

Lesson 106

1. It happens again! Read Judges 16:5-22.
2. Why does he tell Delilah the secret even though it is obvious that she's helping the Philistines?
3. Again, the strongest man is weakened by a woman.
4. Check your answers.

Lesson 107

1. Read Judges 17.
2. What's wrong in this story? Micah's mother says the silver is for the Lord. But what does she say to do with it?
3. What was a Levite's job, do you remember?
4. What does the Levite in this story decide to do?
5. Israel has lost its way. They say they are the following the Lord, but they are all doing it in their own way and not following Him at all!
6. Israel just gets worse and worse. Then a sin is revealed that everyone agrees is so bad that they all unite together to fight against those who committed it and together they clean up Israel and turn back to God.
7. Check your answers.

Lesson 108

1. Read Ruth 1:1-16.
2. Who are Ruth and Naomi?
3. Check your answer.

Lesson 109

1. Read Ruth 2:8-23.
2. Ruth goes to collect grain from a field so that she and Naomi have food to eat. God sends her to a field of a relative of Naomi's. He blesses her in return for how she has cared for Naomi. Naomi recognizes that God has not abandoned her, that He is caring for her.

Lesson 110

1. Read Ruth 4:1-12.
2. This is like a court scene. In the previous chapter Ruth reminds Boaz of the Jewish way of relatives obtaining the property and wives of the deceased in order to continue the family of the deceased. Boaz makes sure that the law is followed. Another relative has the first right to the land, but he doesn't want the obligation.
3. What is the outcome?
4. They have a child and Ruth becomes the great-grandmother of the future King David.
5. Check your answers.

Lesson 111

1. Guess who the book of 1 Samuel is about? It starts with a woman named Hannah who has no children. She is at the house of the Lord at one of the times of sacrifice. She is crying. She promises the Lord that if she has a son, she will dedicate him to the Lord. The priest, Eli, sees her and tells her that she will receive whatever she is asking for. Hannah believes him and is soon pregnant.
2. Read 1 Samuel 2:12-26 and 30-36.
3. Eli's sons did may evil things. What is one of them?
4. What's going to happen to them?
5. God says He's going to raise up a new priest. Who do you think it's going to be?
6. Check your answers.

Lesson 112

1. Read 1 Samuel 3.
2. Who calls to Samuel?
3. Who does Samuel think is calling to him?
4. What does Samuel grow up to be?
5. Check your answers.

Lesson 113

1. The Israelites are fighting the Philistines. They are losing. So, they have an idea…
2. Read 1 Samuel 4:4-18.
3. What do the Israelites bring into camp?
4. What happens to the ark?
5. What happens to Eli's sons?
6. What happens to Eli?
7. Check your answers.

Lesson 114

1. Read 1 Samuel 5.
2. I think this is a funny story. Where do the Philistines put the ark?
3. What did they find in the morning?
4. What else happens to the Philistines?
5. They decide to give the ark back to Israelites and send it to them with a sacrifice.
6. Check your answers.

Lesson 115

1. Read 1 Samuel 8.
2. What does Israel want?
3. Why is that wrong?
4. What is the problem with kings?
5. Read 1 Samuel 10:17-24.
6. Who is chosen king?
7. What makes Saul different?
8. Check your answers.

Lesson 116

1. Read 1 Samuel 12.
2. This is a little review of Israel's history. What sin do they realize they have committed?
3. What is the only way to avoid future disaster for Israel?
4. Check your answers.

Lesson 117

1. Read 1 Samuel 13:1-14.
2. I don't know how long it has been since Saul has been king. It's not the end of his reign though. The first verse there just tells how long altogether that he is king.
3. What does Saul do wrong?
4. What is the punishment?
5. Check your answers.

Lesson 118

1. Read 1 Samuel 15:1-23.
2. What did Saul do wrong?
3. Saul said that he didn't obey because he wanted animals to sacrifice to God. He wanted to do a "good" thing. What does Samuel say is better than sacrifice?
4. Samuel tells him his kingdom is taken away and given to another.
5. Check your answers.

Lesson 119

1. Read 1 Samuel 16.

2. Who did Jesse probably think was God's chosen?
3. How does God choose someone?
4. How does David end up in Saul's palace?
5. Check your answers.

Lesson 120

1. Read 1 Samuel 17:12-58.
2. How is David again in the king's presence and gaining recognition in the kingdom?

Lesson 121

1. Read 1 Samuel 18:1-9, 20-30.
2. What do the people say about Saul and David's success on the battlefield?
3. How is Saul feeling about David?
4. Who does David marry?
5. Check your answers.

Lesson 122

1. In chapter 19 Saul tries to kill David. His jealousy is controlling him. Do you remember anyone else who wanted to kill someone because of jealousy?
2. In chapter 20 we read about what a close friendship David has with Saul's son, Jonathan. Jonathan would be the natural next king because he is the eldest son of Saul. Yet even though he realizes David might be king instead, he is not the one who is jealous. He loves David and helps him by telling him he needs to leave because Saul is going to keep trying to kill David. David runs away.
3. In the next chapters, David is helped by some priests and fights some Philistines and wins. Saul kills the priests for helping David and continues to chase David even though he is fighting on Israel's side against the Philistines.
4. Read 1 Samuel 24.
5. How does David get a chance to kill Saul?
6. Why doesn't David kill Saul?
7. Check your answers.

Lesson 123

1. David marries two more women. He is leading a band of 600 men. David gets the chance to kill Saul again, but he doesn't do it, again. David is living among the Philistines. The Philistines are going to attack Israel. Saul wanted to ask the Lord what would happen, as he normally would seek from the Lord before a battle, but the Lord will not answer him. So Saul gets an idea to ask Samuel, but Samuel had died. Saul, according to the Law of God, had gotten rid of all spiritists and psychics — people who say they can talk to the dead.
2. Read 1 Samuel 28:3-24.
3. Anyone who does this kind of work with spirits is supposed to be killed. The woman fears for her life.

4. There are fake psychics who make things up and tell people what they want to hear. Horoscopes and fortune cookies are forms of this. Even if they are meaningless, I think it's best to avoid them because Satan can use them to try and get you to think a certain way.
5. There are real psychics who serve Satan and can communicate with demons. Demons can see things in the world now and know things from the past. They use those truths to convince people that the psychic really knows what she's talking about. Then Satan can lie about what will happen in the future to control that person's decisions and actions. Only God knows the future. Satan knows nothing of the future except what is written in the Bible.
6. God allows a special circumstance. The woman gets a message from Samuel. Samuel gives one last prophecy, that Saul will die that day.

Lesson 124

1. I'm going to tell you what happens over the next several chapters. Saul and Jonathan are killed in battle against the Philistines. David is made king in Hebron and rules over Judah, but the leader of Saul's army makes one of Saul's sons king over the rest of Israel. The land of Israel is split. The two sides war for seven years. David grows stronger and stronger and the other side grows weaker and weaker. Finally, Israel is united under king David.
2. Read 2 Samuel 5:1-5.
3. How long will David rule over Israel?
4. Check your answers.

Lesson 125

1. Read 2 Samuel 6:1-15.
2. What were they bringing to Jerusalem?
3. Why was David scared of it?
4. What does David do to celebrate?
5. Check your answers.

Lesson 126

1. Read 2 Samuel 7:1-17.
2. Just like God made a covenant promise with Abraham that his people forever would be God's people, God makes a covenant with David and promises that his son will rule after him and that David's kingdom will be established forever through his descendants. God says he will punish David's son, who will disobey, but He will not remove His love like He did from Saul. David does not understand that his firstborn son is not the one who will be king after him, nor does he understand that the everlasting kingdom will be a heavenly kingdom established by the Messiah.
3. Who is the prophet that delivered the message?
4. What did David want to do?
5. Who will build it?
6. Check your answers.

Lesson 127

1. Read 2 Samuel 9.

2. Usually a new king wants to kill everyone from the previous royal family so that there is no threat to his throne. Why does David want to show kindness to someone from Saul's family?
3. Who does he honor?
4. Check your answers.

Lesson 128

1. Read 2 Samuel 11.
2. What sins does David commit?
3. This chapter tells us Bathsheba's father's name. We can read several chapters later that his father, Bathsheba's grandfather, was one of David's advisors, someone David trusted to give him advice. He gave perfect advice. After he realizes what has happened, he leaves David and works for someone else who wants to be king in David's place. That story is coming next.
4. Check your answers.

Lesson 129

1. Read 2 Samuel 12:1-24.
2. Who does God use to confront David about his sin?
3. What happens to Bathsheba's baby?
4. What do they name their next son?
5. Check your answers.

Lesson 130

1. Read 2 Samuel 13:23-31 and 33-38.
2. Who killed whom?
3. Who were those men?
4. Things are never going to be right again since David sinned.
5. Check your answers.

Lesson 131

1. Read 2 Samuel 15:1-14.
2. After several years, Absalom, David's son, starts planning his move to become king. He was David's oldest son, so he expected he was to be the next king. What does he do?
3. What does David do?
4. Check your answers.

Lesson 132

1. Read 2 Samuel 16:23 and 2 Samuel 17:1-14.
2. Ahithophel was David's advisor and became a traitor and joined Absalom. He always gave perfect advice.
3. Hushai was a servant of David's pretending to help Absalom. David sent him to keep Absalom from following Ahithophel's advice.
4. Whose advice does Absalom take?

5. Whose side is the Lord on? [Hint[12]]
6. If we know whose side the Lord is on, then we know the outcome. Who is going to win and be king?
7. Check your answers.

Lesson 133

1. Read 2 Samuel 24:1-17.
2. What was David's sin?
3. It may not seem like a sin, but we read that David felt guilty about it. He knew it was wrong. He wanted to know his strength, as if he knew what he could rely on in battle. He was acting as if he'd forgotten that with God on your side, you can fight with no army at all, and still win!
4. God had reason to punish Israel and this is how he does it. What punishment does David choose?
5. David prays to God and the plague ends. He was right that he could rely on God's mercy.
6. Check your answers.

Lesson 134

1. Read 1 Kings 1:28-40. We've entered a new book, 1 Kings. What's it going to be about?
2. Who is going to be king after David?
3. Whose son is Solomon?
4. He is not David's oldest son. Again, God is choosing who will be king and is not following the custom of the day, where the eldest son would become king.
5. Check your answers.

Lesson 135

1. King David has died and Solomon is ruling as king. Read 1 Kings 3:1-15.
2. God offers Solomon anything he wants. What does he ask for?
3. What does God give him?
4. Check your answers.

Lesson 136

1. Read 1 Kings 4:29-34.
2. Read 1 Kings 5:1-12.
3. What do these two examples show?
4. Check your answers.

Lesson 137

1. Solomon works for 13 years to finish building the temple. Then he gathered everyone together to dedicate the temple to the Lord. You are going to read his prayer at the dedication.
2. Read 1 Kings 8:22-53.
3. What do you think is the main thing he asks for?

---

[12] verse 14

4. Check your answers.

Lesson 138

1. Read 1 Kings 10:14-29.
2. What did Solomon have?
3. What's wrong with all this stuff he got for himself? Read the portion of the law that Solomon forgot in Deuteronomy 17:16-17.
4. Is Solomon in trouble?
5. Check your answers.

Lesson 139

1. Read 1 Kings 11:1-14, and 23-26.
2. What caused Solomon to worship other gods?
3. What is going to happen because he disobeyed and worshiped other gods?
4. Check your answers.

Lesson 140

1. Read 1 Kings 12:1-20.
2. Rehoboam does not have his father's wisdom. What foolish mistake does he make?
3. Everyone leaves Rehoboam. He is left ruling only in Judah. Who is ruling over the rest of the tribes of Israel?
4. From now on it will talk about Judah and Israel, these two portions of former Israel. They will be against each other now.
5. Check your answers.

Lesson 141

1. Jeroboam is king over Israel.
2. Rehoboam is king over Judah.
3. The nation of Israel has been torn in half and they are constantly at war with each other. A long line of kings takes the throne in each place. By far, most of the kings are evil. Read the list of kings below. Try and pay attention to whether the king is in Israel or in Judah. Also, pay attention to anyone who is a good king.
4. Who was the one good king?
5. The last we read, Ahab, married to Jezebel, was king in Israel.
6. Check your answers.

1 Kings 14:21-22

Rehoboam King of Judah

²¹ Rehoboam was king in Judah. He was the son of Solomon. Rehoboam was 41 years old when he became king. He ruled for 17 years in Jerusalem. It was the city the Lord had chosen out of all the cities in the tribes of Israel. He wanted to put his Name there. Rehoboam's mother was Naamah from Ammon.

[22] The people of Judah did what was evil in the sight of the Lord. The sins they had committed made the Lord angry. The Lord was angry because they refused to worship only him. They did more to make him angry than their people who lived before them had done.

1 Kings 15:1-4

Abijah King of Judah

15 Abijah became king of Judah. It was in the 18th year of Jeroboam's rule over Israel. Jeroboam was the son of Nebat. [2] Abijah ruled in Jerusalem for three years. His mother's name was Maakah. She was Abishalom's daughter.
[3] Abijah committed all the sins his father had committed before him. Abijah didn't obey the Lord his God with all his heart. He didn't do what King David had done. [4] But the Lord still kept the lamp of Abijah's kingdom burning brightly in Jerusalem. He did it by giving him a son to be the next king after him. He also did it by making Jerusalem strong. The Lord did those things because of David.

1 Kings 15:9-11

Asa King of Judah

[9] Asa became king of Judah. It was in the 20th year that Jeroboam was king of Israel. [10] Asa ruled in Jerusalem for 41 years. His grandmother's name was Maakah. She was Abishalom's daughter.
[11] Asa did what was right in the sight of the Lord. That's what King David had done.

1 Kings 15:25-26

Nadab King of Israel

[25] Nadab became king of Israel. It was in the second year that Asa was king of Judah. Nadab ruled over Israel for two years. He was the son of Jeroboam. [26] Nadab did what was evil in the sight of the Lord. He lived the way his father had lived. He committed the same sin his father Jeroboam had caused Israel to commit.

1 Kings 15:33-34

Baasha King of Israel

[33] Baasha became king of Israel in Tirzah. It was in the third year that Asa was king of Judah. Baasha ruled for 24 years. He was the son of Ahijah. [34] Baasha did what was evil in the sight of the Lord. He lived the way Jeroboam had lived. He committed the same sin Jeroboam had caused Israel to commit.

1 Kings 16:8

Elah King of Israel

[8] Elah became king of Israel. It was in the 26th year that Asa was king of Judah. Elah ruled in Tirzah for two years. He was the son of Baasha.

1 Kings 16:13

[13] Baasha and his son Elah had committed all kinds of sin. They had also caused Israel to commit the same sins. So Israel made the Lord very angry. They did it by worshiping worthless statues of gods. The Lord is the God of Israel.

1 Kings 16:29-33

Ahab King of Israel

[29] Ahab became king of Israel. It was in the 38th year that Asa was king of Judah. Ahab ruled over Israel in Samaria for 22 years. He was the son of Omri. [30] Ahab, the son of Omri, did what was evil in the sight of the Lord. He did more evil things than any of the kings who had ruled before him. [31] He thought it was only a small thing to commit the sins Jeroboam, the son of Nebat, had committed. Ahab also married Jezebel. She was Ethbaal's daughter. Ethbaal was king of the people of Sidon. Ahab began to serve the god named Baal and worship him. [32] He set up an altar to honor Baal. He set it up in the temple of Baal that he built in Samaria. [33] Ahab also made a pole used to worship the female god named Asherah. He made the Lord very angry. Ahab did more to make him angry than all the kings of Israel had done before him. The Lord is the God of Israel.

Lesson 142

1. While Ahab is king in Israel, a new prophet comes on the scene, Elijah. In this chapter we read a prophecy and about several miracles.
2. Read 1 Kings 17.
3. What is the prophecy he makes?
4. How does God provide for him at first?
5. When the brook dried up, where did God send Elijah?
6. What miracles did the widow receive?
7. Check your answers.

Lesson 143

1. A few years have passed and Ahab is still king in Israel. Read 1 Kings 18:16-46. This is a long but famous story.
2. Tell the story of the Mount Carmel challenge.
3. Afterwards, Elijah goes and prays. What happens?
4. Ahab gets in his chariot and rides off. Elijah starts running. Who's faster?
5. Check your answers.

Lesson 144

1. Jezebel wants to kill Elijah. He runs away. God sends an angel to Elijah to feed him to prepare for a journey. God sends him far away, to Mount Sinai (see the map on the next page).
2. Read 1 Kings 19:9-18.
3. God comes to Elijah. He doesn't come in the power of an earthquake or a fire. What does he come and speak in?
4. Who will be God's prophet after Elijah?
5. The Israelites are going to be punished for worshiping Baal. How many will the Lord keep safe because they never worshiped another god?

6. We call that the remnant. There is always a remnant, a group of true believers. Never feel like you are alone in loving and serving God. God always has a people that He has kept for himself.
7. Check your answers.

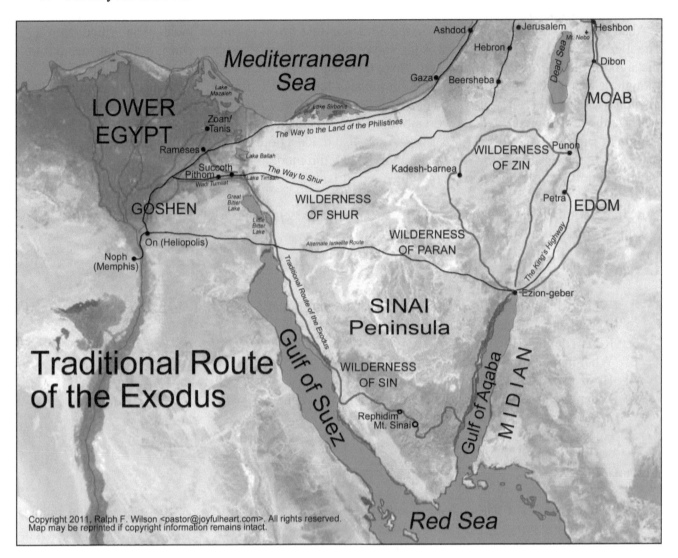

Lesson 145

1. The king of Israel, Ahab, and the king of Judah, Jehoshaphat, came together in an alliance to fight against Aram. Jehoshaphat asks that they inquire of the Lord before battle. Ahab has many false prophets who all say that he will have success. Jehoshaphat insists on having a prophet of the Lord come. They send for Micaiah.
2. Read 1 Kings 22:12-35.
3. Micaiah describes a heavenly meeting. What was God looking for?
4. What was the plan to get Ahab to Aram?
5. How is Ahab killed?
6. Check your answers.

Lesson 146

1. Read 2 Kings 2:1-14.

2. How does Elisha know he has received what he asked for?
3. What is the first miracle Elisha does now that the Spirit of God is on him?
4. Check your answers.

Lesson 147

1. Read 2 Kings 4:1-7, 38-44.
2. Tell someone the three miracle stories you read about. Here are reminders: oil, stew, bread.

Lesson 148

1. Read 2 Kings 5:1-16.
2. Who was healed of leprosy?
3. He almost wasn't healed, why?
4. The dipping in water wasn't important. That didn't do anything. It was the act of obeying that showed faith in the Word of God that was important.
5. What does Elisha say when Naaman wants to pay for being healed?
6. Check your answers.

Lesson 149

1. Read 2 Kings 6:1-23.
2. What does God allow Elisha's servant to see?
3. Check your answers.

Lesson 150

1. The Israelites are under siege. Do you remember what a siege is? It's when the enemy army has you surrounded. You wait and see who can last the longest. The Israelites have run out of food. Everyone is starving. If anyone had any bread, it would sell for so much money because everyone would want it. There is a prophecy in the chapter you will read today that flour and grain would sell cheaply.
2. Read 2 Kings 7.
3. How many Arameans (air-a-me-ins) were killed when God gave the victory to the Israelites?
4. How did God give food to the Israelites?
5. Check your answers.

Lesson 151

1. Read 2 Kings 8:1-6.
2. How does God make a way for the woman to receive her land back?
3. There is a list of kings that all do wrong and are eventually killed. Here we read about Jehu. He was a king of Israel. He wasn't one of the "good" kings, but God gave him the job of destroying what was left of Ahab's family.
4. Read 2 Kings 10:28-35.
5. Next we will read about a new king in Judah. Joash is only 7 years old when he becomes king. A priest, Jehoiada, is leading Israel on Joash's behalf, and teaching Joash the right way to live.
6. Check your answers.

Lesson 152

1. Read 2 Kings 12:1-12.
2. What did Joash accomplish?
3. Check your answers.

Lesson 153

1. Elisha dies and there is a long line of kings who do evil. Joash's son does okay for awhile as king of Judah, but everyone else does "what is evil in the eyes of the Lord."
2. Read 2 Kings 17:1-23.
3. What is Israel's punishment for their constant sinning, turning to other gods?
4. Check your answers.

Lesson 154

1. Read 2 Kings 18:1-8.
2. Who was Judah's next "good" king?
3. Assyria is ready to attack Judah.
4. Read 2 Kings 19:9-19.
5. The king of Assyria says Judah's God can do nothing. Hezekiah prays. What do you think will happen?
6. Read 2 Kings 20:1-11.
7. Does Judah defeat Assyria?
8. Is Hezekiah healed?
9. Check your answers.

Lesson 155

1. Read 2 Kings 21.
2. Hezekiah did not do a good job of training up his son. Granted, he was only twelve when Hezekiah died. His mother must have been a very bad influence. What is Hezekiah's son's name? He was the worst king ever.
3. Check your answers.

Lesson 156

1. Read about Manasseh's grandson. His mother must have been a very good influence.
2. Read 2 Kings 22.
3. What is his name?
4. What is found in the temple?
5. Check your answers.

Lesson 157

1. Read 2 Kings 23:1-30.
2. When Josiah hears the law, he humbles himself and seeks the Lord and determines to follow the law. What are some of the things that he does?

3. Check your answers.

Lesson 158

1. Read 2 Kings 25:1-12.
2. Which king takes Jerusalem into exile (forces them to leave their land)?
3. Who gets to stay home?
4. Check your answers.

Lesson 159

1. The next book of the Bible is Chronicles. There is a first and second Chronicles. A chronicle is a history. This is a history record of what happened. It starts with a genealogy, a list of names, starting with Adam and listing their children down through thousands of years.
2. It also retells some of the stories we just read. When it retells stories, it often adds in more detail than we read before.
3. Read this story from when Rehoboam was king, 2 Chronicles 12:1-12.
4. Why does God not destroy them?
5. What lesson does God say He wants to teach them?
6. Check your answers.

Lesson 160

1. Read 2 Chronicles 20:5-30.
2. This is one of my favorite chapters in the Bible. A huge army rises up against Judah. Jehoshaphat prays. The army of Judah goes out singing and by the time they get to the battle, the other army is already dead. They didn't have to fight.
3. What weapons did the army of Judah fight with?
4. Check your answers.

Lesson 161

1. Read 2 Chronicles 26.
2. Uzziah was one of the good kings of Judah. What led to his getting leprosy?
3. Check your answers.

Lesson 162

1. Read 2 Chronicles 32:24-33.
2. You've read about Hezekiah getting sick and healed before. Here is another perspective as to what happened. What sin was he guilty of and then repented of?
3. Why did God leave him?
4. Check your answers.

Lesson 163

1. We are moving into a new book now. Israel no longer has a king. They have been conquered.
2. Read Ezra 1.

3. What king of Persia decides to rebuild the temple of the Lord?
4. Look at the map showing Persia during Cyrus' rule. The kingdom expanded over time. Its growth is shown by each darker area on the map. He says that God has given him all the kingdoms on earth. That was the "whole world" to them.
5. Who was in control of Cyrus building the temple?
6. Check your answers.

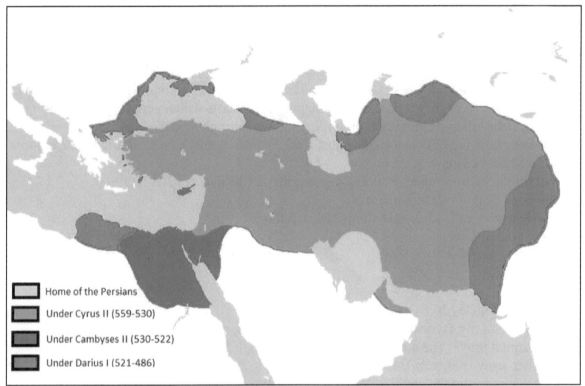

Home of the Persians

Under Cyrus II (559-530)

Under Cambyses II (530-522)

Under Darius I (521-486)

Lesson 164

1. Read Ezra 3:7-13.
2. Everyone was giving money. The workers were working. Who was happy when the foundation of the temple was laid?
3. Who was sobbing when the foundation was laid?
4. Check your answers.

Lesson 165

1. Enemies of the Jews try to stop them from rebuilding the temple. They try to discourage them. They try to get laws in place to stop them. Here is how the Israelites respond and how God helps them.
2. Read Ezra 5.
3. King Darius responds that they should continue their work.
4. Many Israelites are allowed to return to Jerusalem.

Lesson 166

1. We are moving into another book, Nehemiah. The Israelites are again turning to God. They have collectively repented of marrying foreign wives who led them astray. Word gets back to Nehemiah about Jerusalem's condition.
2. Read Nehemiah 1.
3. What happened to Jerusalem?
4. What does Nehemiah do when he hears the news of Jerusalem?
5. Check your answers.

Lesson 167

1. Read Nehemiah 2.
2. The King gives Nehemiah time off to go see to rebuilding his ancestral city of Jerusalem. Some people are not happy. What is Nehemiah confident of?
3. Check your answers.

Lesson 168

1. Read Nehemiah 4.
2. How did God frustrate their enemies?
3. Check your answers.

Lesson 169

1. Read Nehemiah 5.
2. Why were the people suffering?
3. Why was Nehemiah a good governor?
4. Check your answers.

Lesson 170

1. Read Nehemiah 6.
2. How are people trying to stop the work?
3. What does Nehemiah do when he is told that people want to kill him?
4. They complete the wall and acknowledge that it was completed because God helped them.
5. Check your answers.

Lesson 171

1. Read Nehemiah 8.
2. There is revival in Jerusalem. They are reading God's law, confessing their sins and committing themselves to following the law and celebrating the Lord's festivals.

Lesson 172

1. Read Esther 1.
2. Tell someone what is happening in the story.

Lesson 173

1. Read Esther 2.
2. Tell someone what is happening in the story.

Lesson 174

1. Read Esther 3.
2. Tell someone what is happening in the story.

Lesson 175

1. Read Esther 4.
2. Tell someone what is happening in the story.

Lesson 176

1. Read Esther 5.
2. Tell someone what is happening in the story.

Lesson 177

1. Read Esther 6.
2. Tell someone what is happening in the story.

Lesson 178

1. Read Esther 7.
2. Tell someone what is happening in the story.

Lesson 179

1. Read Esther 8.
2. Tell someone what is happening in the story.

Lesson 180

1. Read Esther 9 and Esther 10.
2. Tell someone how the story ends.

Worksheets

Lesson 9

C   _____

O   _____

M   _____

P   _____

A   _____

S   _____

S   _____

I   _____

O   _____

N   _____

Lesson 30

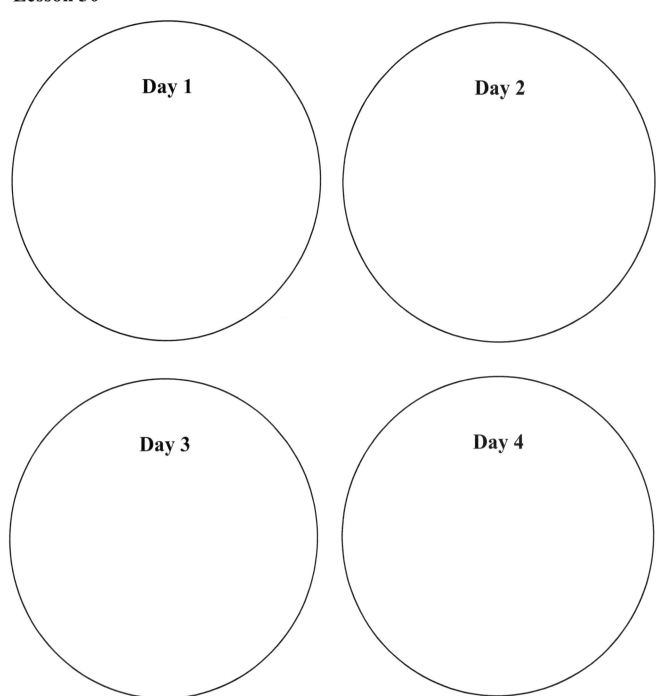

Day 1

Day 2

Day 3

Day 4

Lesson 31

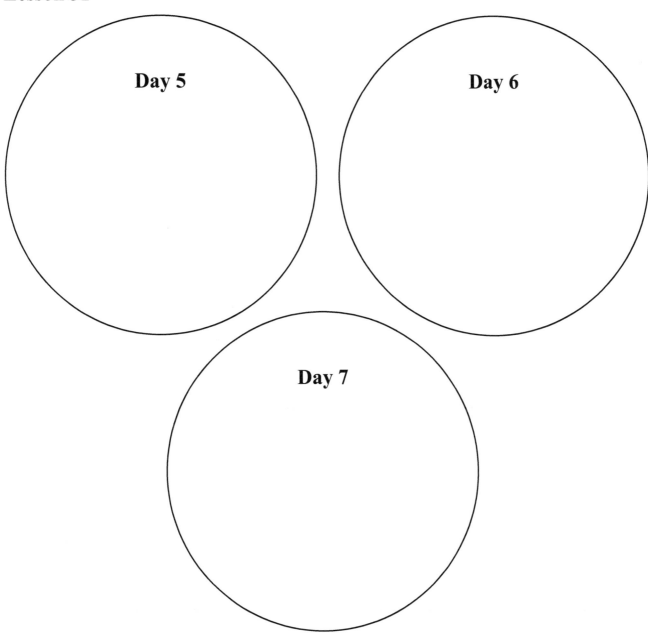

Day 5

Day 6

Day 7

Lesson 74

1. _____

2. _____

3. _____

4. _____

5. _____

6. _____

7. _____

8. _____

9. _____

10. _____

Answers

Lesson 2

1. Micah 5:2 God spoke about it hundreds of years before.
2. God warned them in a dream.

Lesson 3

1. They need to show that they have repented and turned away from doing sin.

Lesson 5

1. It can make you happy because you will receive a reward in heaven, and you can know you are experiencing the same as Jesus and the other prophets.

Lesson 7

1. obey God's word

Lesson 8

1. Jesus healed someone, someone came to Jesus asking for healing, they both believed that Jesus could heal
2. Jesus touched the one man to heal him and the other he healed just by speaking that he was healed, one man was a Jew and the other was a Gentile (not a Jew), one expected Jesus to heal the other wasn't sure if Jesus was willing to heal him

Lesson 11

1. He would prepare the way for Jesus to come. He did that by teaching people to repent and turn away from their sins.

Lesson 12

1. breaking the Sabbath, the command to not work one day a week

Lesson 18

1. Christians must forgive each other and those who seek forgiveness from them.

Lesson 19

1. He was still rich. He was keeping his money for himself.

Lesson 20

1. He came to serve others.

Lesson 21

1. a den of robbers

Lesson 22

1. The king invites guests to his son's wedding dinner. They don't want to come. So, the king has his servants invite others. They come, but one is kicked out because he's not wearing wedding clothes.
2. The king is God and his son is Jesus.
3. The Bible talks about how we are cleaned by the blood of Jesus and how He will dress us in white, make us pure from all sin. This man didn't believe in Jesus. He hadn't had his sin forgiven. He wasn't welcome in heaven and is thrown into hell.

Lesson 23

1. hypocrites, proud

Lesson 24

1. Don't be alarmed.

Lesson 26

1. His choice was to be obedient. This is what God had chosen from the beginning.

Lesson 27

1. Crucify him!
2. Hosanna to the Son of David! Blessed is the one who comes in the name of the Lord!

Lesson 28

1. If there were asleep, they couldn't know who rolled away the stone and took the body. And, guards would never sleep on the job because they would be killed if they did and allowed something to happen.

Lesson 32

1. the serpent
2. Eve

Lesson 33

1. grab him
2. sin
3. Some answers: avoid temptation-get away from it, pray and praise, ask for help, decide with all your heart and mind that you always want to obey God's word, fear God

Lesson 34

1. verses 6, 13
2. verses 9, 22

Lesson 35

1. 7 days
2. Noah and his wife, his three sons and their wives, 2 of every kind of unclean animal, 7 of every clean animal, 7 of every kind of bird
3. 150 days

Lesson 36

1. to sacrifice as an offering
2. meat
3. The rainbow is the reminder of God's promise to never again destroy the world by a flood.

Lesson 37

1. Abram is Lot's uncle
2. to leave his home and go to the land where God would show him
3. that from him would come a great nation and that all the nations of the world would be blessed because of him

Lesson 38

1. Sodom
2. The men were evil and sinning against God.

Lesson 39

1. That he will have as many children as the stars in the sky. Children here means descendants, meaning his children's children and his children's children's children's children, etc.
2. He believed.
3. They are going to be slaves in a foreign country.

Lesson 40

1. Abraham and Sarah
2. Yes! Abraham will have a child when he is 100 and Sarah when she is 90.

Lesson 41

1. God is planning on destroying Sodom and Gomorrah. Abraham is asking him not to if there are righteous people in the city.
2. no
3. She turns into a salt statue.

4. It's important to obey the word of the Lord. God listens to prayer and it can make a big difference.

Lesson 42

1. Abraham obeyed.

Lesson 44

1. Esau and Jacob
2. Abraham
3. He gave up his rights as the first-born son.

Lesson 45

1. He saw a stairway to heaven and angels going up and down them and the Lord at the top of the stairs.
2. The promise He gave Abraham that he would have many descendants and they would be given the land he was on and that the world will be blessed through them.
3. If God took care of Him on his journey, then he would take Him as his God and give him a tithe, a tenth of everything that he had.

Lesson 46

1. 4
2. Judah
3. 12

Lesson 47

1. runs away with his family and belongings
2. steals the household gods

Lesson 48

1. that grain and stars bowed down to him, meaning his brothers would bow down to him
2. They were jealous because Joseph was their father's favorite.
3. Reuben
4. Potiphar, Pharaoh's official

Lesson 49

1. He blessed everything Joseph did.
2. He was in charge of everything in Potiphar's home.
3. He is thrown in jail.

Lesson 50

1. the royal cupbearer and the baker
2. Joseph told them what their dreams meant, and he was right.

Lesson 51

1. Seven fat cows and seven heads of grain mean there will be seven years of lots of food and wealth. Seven skinny cows and seven bad heads of grain that eat the good ones mean that seven years when there won't be enough will come and "eat up" anything extra from the years when there was plenty.

Lesson 52

1. He stored up grain.
2. He sold them grain.

Lesson 53

1. all of Joseph's brothers except Benjamin
2. spying
3. They bowed down to them.

Lesson 55

1. silver cup to make it look like he stole it
2. Judah

Lesson 56

1. God

Lesson 57

1. that He would be in Egypt with them and that He would bring them out again
2. the part of Egypt called Goshen

Lesson 58

1. that Joseph would do something to get back at them
2. because he was in Egypt he was able to interpret the Pharaoh's dream and store up food to give the people during the famine to keep them from starving

Lesson 59

1. He made them slaves and ordered that all the boy babies be killed.

Lesson 60

   1. by killing the Egyptian

Lesson 62

   1. He gives him miracles to perform, including a staff that turns into a snake, and he sends his brother Aaron to speak for him.

Lesson 63

   1. He said no and increased their work.

Lesson 64

   1. turn the Nile into blood

Lesson 65

   1. He kept the plague of flies from Goshen, which is where the Israelites lived.

Lesson 66

   1. He killed the farm animals of the Egyptians.
   2. None of the animals belonging to the Hebrews, Israelites, died.

Lesson 67

   1. darkness
   2. They will have light.
   3. Pharaoh will never see his face again.

Lesson 68

   1. The first born of all the Egyptians died.

Lesson 69

   1. Pharaoh changed his mind and sent his army after the Israelites. God made a way for them to escape by opening a pathway of dry land through the sea, but the water crashed down on the Egyptian army.

Lesson 70

   1. He tells them to obey Him.

Lesson 71

1. They grumbled, again.
2. quail meat in the evening and bread in the morning.

Lesson 72

1. They questioned, "Is the Lord among us or not?" They questioned if God had abandoned them and stopped taking care of them.
2. He had to keep up his arms and his staff.

Lesson 77

1. What I saw that seemed strange and unusual is that they saw God, at least his feet. Also, they put blood on everybody.

Lesson 78

1. They built an idol, a statue to worship as god.
2. He sent a plague.

Lesson 83

1. He says that the land they live on is really His. He says they are just renting the land. They shouldn't act like they own it.

Lesson 85

1. They complained.
2. God sent a fire and a plague.

Lesson 86

1. sounds like they were prideful and jealous
2. She got leprosy.
3. He was more humble than everyone and God spoke to him plainly face to face.

Lesson 87

1. Caleb
2. They say the people there are so big and their cities have walls around them.

Lesson 88

1. They want a new leader. They don't want to fight.
2. They want to kill them.
3. They can't enter the Promised Land. Anyone 20 years old and up will have to die in the desert. The Israelites will wander in the desert for 40 years instead of entering into the Promised Land.

Lesson 90

1. He has the leader of each tribe write his name on a staff and place it in the tabernacle. In the morning Aaron's staff had budded, blossomed and produced almonds. His staff was placed in the tabernacle as a reminder to everyone.

Lesson 91

1. Speak to the rock and water will come out.
2. He strikes the rock like God had had him do 40 years earlier.

Lesson 92

1. He sends a destroying angel to block his path.
2. His donkey stays away from the angel.
3. The talking donkey!

Lesson 93

1. Joshua

Lesson 95

1. He says you can choose between life and death. If they obey God, they will live. If they disobey God, they will die.

Lesson 96

1. The priests stand in the water carrying the ark of the covenant, and the water stops flowing and heaps up in a pile, leaving the ground dry for the Israelites to cross.

Lesson 97

1. Obey God! Did I trick you? Yes, they had to march 7 days and play trumpets and shout, but the marching and shouting doesn't make walls fall down; only God could have done that. Their obedience showed their faith in Him to do it!

Lesson 98

1. They are defeated and chased away.
2. Someone had disobeyed God's command not to take anything from Jericho for themselves.
3. Achan

Lesson 99

1. Sun, stand still until we have the complete victory.

Lesson 100

1. God sent hornets to get the others to leave the land.
2. that they will serve the Lord

Lesson 101

1. They disobey. They serve other gods. They break their word.
2. God will no longer drive out the nations before them. Other peoples will still live in their land.
3. He will raise up a judge to deliver them from their enemies.

Lesson 102

1. Deborah

Lesson 103

1. They disobeyed.
2. They were taken over by the Midianites.
3. It's who Moses lived with when he ran away from Egypt.
4. Unsure. He asks God to show him twice that He really was going to use Gideon to do this big job. God does what Gideon asks.

Lesson 104

1. 300
2. Each one carried a torch and a trumpet, so it looked like there were 300 light carriers and it sounded like there were 300 trumpet blowers all coming before what must be a really big army!

Lesson 105

1. He tore a lion apart.
2. his wife
3. She wore him down with nagging.

Lesson 106

1. She wore him down with constant nagging.

Lesson 107

1. make an idol
2. They were in charge of the temple and the sacrifices.
3. He becomes a priest for the idol.

Lesson 108

1. Naomi is an Israelite who left Israel because of famine. She returned to Israel after her husband died. Her two daughters-in-law are with her. One goes back to Moab. but Ruth decides to stay with Naomi and become a follower of the God of Israel.

Lesson 110

1. Boaz agrees to take Ruth as his wife.

Lesson 111

1. The biggest is that they didn't fear the Lord. They stole meat that people were bringing to sacrifice to God.
2. They will both die on the same day.

Lesson 112

1. the Lord
2. Eli
3. a prophet

Lesson 113

1. the ark
2. It is captured.
3. They are killed in battle. They both die in one day just like Samuel had prophesied.
4. He falls over and dies when he hears the ark has been captured.

Lesson 114

1. in one of their temples, next to a statue of Dagon, one of their gods
2. the statue was lying face down before the ark like he was honoring and worshiping God
3. They are plagued with tumors.

Lesson 115

1. a king
2. because God is their king
3. They will demand things from the people for themselves.
4. Saul
5. He's taller than everyone else.

Lesson 116

1. asking for a king
2. They and their king have to obey God.

Lesson 117

1. He presents the offering to God instead of a priest doing it.
2. He is told that his kingdom won't last, that it will be given to another.

Lesson 118

1. He didn't obey God.
2. to obey is better than sacrifice

Lesson 119

1. his oldest son
2. not by appearance but by their heart
3. He is chosen to play the harp for him.

Lesson 121

1. Saul has killed thousands and David tens of thousands.
2. He is jealous. He thinks David will take his kingdom.
3. Saul's daughter.

Lesson 122

1. Cain and some of Joseph's brothers
2. Saul is going to the bathroom in a cave where David is hiding.
3. He wouldn't hurt the one the Lord anointed. He is not in rebellion against the king at all. He would be happy to serve king Saul if he weren't trying to kill him!

Lesson 124

1. 40 years

Lesson 125

1. the ark of the covenant
2. Someone touched it and was killed.
3. dances

Lesson 126

1. Nathan
2. build a house for the Lord
3. his son

Lesson 127

1. for Jonathan's sake

2. Mephibosheth; try and say it out loud!

Lesson 128

1. adultery–treating another woman as if she were his wife, and murdering Uriah

Lesson 129

1. Nathan
2. dies
3. Solomon

Lesson 130

1. Absalom killed Amnon.
2. David's sons

Lesson 131

1. He starts acting as judge and then gets a group together to declare that he is king in the city of Hebron.
2. flees the palace

Lesson 132

1. Hushai
2. David's
3. David. Absalom and Ahithophel die.

Lesson 133

1. taking a census, counting his army
2. a plague

Lesson 134

1. Solomon
2. David and Bathsheba's

Lesson 135

1. wisdom, understanding, knowing what is right and wrong
2. wisdom and understanding and honor and riches

Lesson 136

1. how God had given him great wisdom

Lesson 137

1. It seems like he is asking, "Hear us when we pray,"

Lesson 138

1. everything! He got so much money, horses and chariots and, as we'll learn, wives.
2. You bet!

Lesson 139

1. His wives worshiped other gods and led him astray, but they couldn't have done that if he hadn't first disobeyed God's command to not marry women from those nations. He also disobeyed the command to not get lots of wives for himself. His disobedience was his downfall.
2. Most of the kingdom will be taken from his son and he will have troubles with people coming against him for the rest of his life.

Lesson 140

1. He doesn't listen to his father's advisors. He listens to his friends who have no wisdom from experience, and he makes the whole nation mad!
2. Jeroboam

Lesson 141

1. Asa, king in Judah

Lesson 142

1. that there will be no dew or rain for the next few years
2. God tells him where there is a source of water and sends ravens to deliver him bread and meat twice a day.
3. to the house of a widow
4. She never ran out of oil and flour to make bread. Her son came back to life.

Lesson 143

1. the drought is ended and it rains
2. Elijah, by the power of God

Lesson 144

1. a gentle whisper
2. Elisha
3. 7000

Lesson 145

1. a way to get Ahab to Aram so he would be killed there
2. put lies in the mouths of his prophets, saying he would be successful
3. Ahab tries to hide, but an arrow "randomly" is shot and strikes him just at the right place and kills him.

Lesson 146

1. He saw Elijah being taken away in a fiery chariot.
2. He strikes the Jordan with his cloak, and it parts so that he can walk across.

Lesson 148

1. Naaman; he wasn't an Israelite.
2. He was proud and didn't think dipping himself in the water was worth it.
3. no way

Lesson 149

1. fiery horses and chariots ready to fight for them

Lesson 150

1. none
2. He scared away the Arameans with the noise of an approaching army. Then the Israelites took all of the belongings of the Arameans.

Lesson 151

1. The king was just hearing about her as she walked in.

Lesson 152

1. repairing the temple

Lesson 153

1. They were sent into exile, had to leave their own country, and they were removed from God's presence. He's no longer with them. What could be worse?

Lesson 154

1. Hezekiah
2. Yes
3. Yes

Lesson 155

1. Manasseh

Lesson 156

1. Josiah
2. scroll containing the law

Lesson 157

1. He got rid of everything and everyone that was for Baal worship. He reinstituted the Passover feast. He also got rid of witchcraft.

Lesson 158

1. Nebuchadnezzar
2. Some of the poorest people get to stay to work the fields.

Lesson 159

1. They aren't destroyed because they humble themselves. They accept that God is right and they are wrong.
2. the difference between serving Him and serving other kings

Lesson 160

1. faith and praise

Lesson 161

1. his pride

Lesson 162

1. pride
2. to test what was in his heart

Lesson 163

1. Cyrus
2. God

Lesson 164

1. everyone, well, all of the Israelites
2. Those who remembered the first temple.

Lesson 166

1. Its wall surrounding the city was broken down.
2. prays

Lesson 167

1. God will give them success.

Lesson 168

1. He let the Israelites learn of their plans to attack, and the Israelites set guards over all of the work.

Lesson 169

1. They had such heavy taxes to pay. They didn't own anything and had to keep paying the owners.
2. He didn't take advantage of his position. He didn't take money and food from people like others had.

Lesson 170

1. They are trying to discourage them. They are making up lies about them revolting against the king.
2. He doesn't run and hide. He prays.

The Easy Peasy All-in-One Homeschool is a free, complete online homeschool curriculum. There are 180 days of ready-to-go assignments for every level and every subject. It's created for your children to work as independently as you want them to. Preschool through high school is available as well as courses ranging from English, math, science and history to art, music, computer, thinking, physical education and health. A daily Bible lesson is offered as well. The mission of Easy Peasy is to enable those to homeschool who otherwise thought they couldn't.

The Genesis Curriculum takes the Bible and turns it into lessons for your homeschool. Daily lessons include Bible reading, memory verse, spelling, handwriting, vocabulary, grammar, Biblical language, science, social studies, writing, and thinking through discussion questions.

The Genesis Curriculum uses a complete book of the Bible for one full year. The curriculum is being made using both Old and New Testament books. Find us online at genesiscurriculum.com to read about the latest developments in this expanding curriculum.

Made in United States
Troutdale, OR
08/18/2023

12172771R00040